Raising a Happy and Healthy Dog

The Best Training Techniques for Well Behaved Puppies and Dogs

Lou Jefferson

Copyrights

Disclaimer and Terms of Use

ISBN: 978-1546444619

Printed in the United States

MAPLEWOOD
– PUBLISHING –

Contents

Introduction

Getting a new puppy is an extremely exciting and life changing thing for the whole family, whether that family is as small as you and your partner, or it is as big as a family of eight. Everyone is always extremely excited when the time comes to bring home the new family member, but with great happiness becomes a great responsibility.

As you are now bringing home that cute, irresistible bundle of fur you need to have a teaching method in place to teach him or her the correct way to not only be your best friend, but to listen to your commands and become obedient. In this book, you will learn different ways and techniques to teach your puppy to be obedient using positive reinforcement.

This specific technique has been scientifically proven to be the most effective way to teach your puppy to love and respect you, and not be scared and fear doing the wrong thing. Puppies are still very young and need your kind, loving care and guidance – as we are still learning to become the best teacher we can be for these cute puppies!

You may ask yourself, how do I stop this puppy from peeing all over the house? How do I teach him not to be so destructive and ruin the expensive furniture? How am I supposed to sleep when she whines all night? How do I teach him to play nice with the other dogs?

It's ok! In my many years of experience, I've discovered these are the most common questions owners ask themselves.

If you wish to know the answer to these questions I encourage you to read on into the depths of this book, where you will not only find yourself learning in great detail about puppy training, but also techniques and methods for controlling the behavior of your cute little puppy using positive reinforcement.

The simpler your commands, the more motivated your pet will be to respond. Save those that are more complex for later. Begin with the basics: sit, heel, stay, and come. Once he has mastered these commands both on and off his leash, move on to more difficult ones. For instance, teach him to "drop it," "go to your place," and "look at me."

Positive reinforcement teaches your dog that good things happen when he does what you want. You will learn to build a loving and trusting relationship

1

with your new family member through praise and rewards, which is infinitely better than one based on punishment and fear.

Puppy training is important for every puppy owner. If you want to have a puppy who will live with you and share in your daily life, you will need to train him so he does not endanger you or the things you consider important in your household.

Puppies are special creatures who grow up to be loyal companions and effective guard dogs. They can bring much joy into your life, especially if you are a dog-loving person. However, there is a need to train your puppy as early as possible so that he will have good behavior when he grows up.

As children need to be trained by their parents early on, puppies also need to be trained so they get to know what is right and wrong, especially with regard to eating, peeing or pooping, relationships, and behavior towards you and the people around you.

Read on, to see how you can get started!

Choosing a Dog

Before considering getting a dog ask yourself, should I get a dog?

Maybe the children want a cute little puppy, and they will not take no for an answer. Are you lonely and want companionship? Are you looking for a guard dog? Be honest with yourself as to the real reason you want a dog. Then you can think about what type is right for you, and will fit comfortably into your lifestyle. Ask yourself the following five questions before you choose.

1) Can I afford a dog?
Here are some facts on the cost of owning a dog. Besides the actual cost of buying one, there are some essential dog supplies you will have to get before bringing him home. You will need water and food bowls, a crate for him to sleep in, a dog collar and leash, toys to keep him occupied, treats, and a grooming kit just to name a few things. There will be the recurring costs of food, pet insurance, worming, and annual visits to the veterinarian for vaccinations and health checks. You may have to pay someone to care for him while you are on holidays.

2) Do you have the time?
A dog is a full-time commitment – seven days a week – and the main thing she needs from you is time. You must walk her no matter what the weather is like, dry, wet, hot, or cold. You will need to bathe and groom your dog properly. If you get a puppy, then quite a lot of time will be involved training her, particularly puppy potty training. You may have to get up earlier in the mornings to take your dog out to relieve herself and exercise. If she was left alone all day, you will have to try to get back home to her or arrange for a dog walker, family member, or friend to take her out for a walk. An energetic type needs lots of exercise, or they can resort to destructive or bad behavior if there is no release for all that energy. You need to spend time interacting with your dog to help form a good bond with her. You have to play with her, train her, and simply enjoy your dog.

3) Will you choose a puppy or an adult?
A puppy can be hard work. They are very time consuming and need lots of attention while growing. Puppies need to play, eat, and relieve themselves a lot. However, you get great pleasure watching your puppy grow, hopefully into a well-trained dog. It is easier to bond with a puppy. An adult dog eats fewer meals and can hold its bladder for longer. It will probably be house trained, but you will know very little about its history. Older dogs take time to settle in, so you will need to spend a lot of time with him to strengthen a bond between

you. If he is an energetic adolescent, you will have your hands full. A lot of adolescent dogs end up in dog shelters as their owners cannot manage them and are no longer interested in keeping them once they have grown out of the cute puppy stage.

4 and 5) Big or small, male or female?
Small dogs eat less so they are cheaper to feed, and they take up less space. A big dog may not be a good choice if you have small children or an elderly relative in the house who might be easily knocked over. Do research on the breed you want, and check for its exercise needs and temperament. Males tend to be bigger than females. They are more likely to be territorial and wander more, looking for a mate. Neutering can lessen this tendency. Females can be very affectionate; this will attract a lot of male dogs in your area. Getting a female spayed cures that problem and stops the risk of unwanted puppies. If you are contemplating buying a dog, then visit a puppy breeder and ask lots of questions about the puppy and its parents. Visit a few times before you make a final decision. You can usually get a shelter dog for free, but there might be a small charge to cover the cost of vaccinations.

There is no doubt a dog can bring lots of pleasure and fun to your life for many years. It can add richness in a way money never can. A dog is forgiving and loves you no matter what. In return, treat your dog with kindness, train him/her well and provide a caring home.

Before You Start, General Tips for Effective Puppy Training

Most puppies can start out with simple methods for training, like accepting praise or learning to wear a collar, when they are only eight weeks old. You can start using basic commands when the puppy reaches 12 weeks of age. If you keep the following tips in mind, you'll be ready for success.

First ensure that you have his attention. Before you begin throwing commands at your puppy, ensure that his attention is focused on you. The goal here is never to give a command that won't be followed by the puppy. You can get his attention by simply saying his name (if he's learned it yet), or a quick snap of the fingers before you give an instruction. Ensure that your dog is facing you and has his attention on you. When you don't make sure that you have his attention first, before giving commands, you are reinforcing the notion that the puppy may obey you or listen to you only when he wants to.

Give him time. You must make sure you are allowing the pup adequate time to react to your command, and let him follow through. Give the command only once, and then give the puppy a chance to obey. The goal of training is to let the puppy learn that he must obey you every single time.

Use short sessions. Start by using short sessions for training that last no longer than 10 minutes. Remember to end these on a note of positivity, making the session fun and engaging for your puppy. The goal here is to have your puppy associate positive experiences with doing what you ask of her. You should also use these sessions as a chance to foster a deeper bond with the dog. Remember that puppies have short attention spans, and they must be focused during a training session. When your puppy is tired or has been trying to learn something new for too long, she doesn't have a chance to use her full abilities.

Have good timing. The best time to do a training session is right before a meal when your dog is a bit hungry. This will allow her to realize that following a command results in getting treats.

Use short commands. Use commands that are short, preferably no longer than one or two words, for any behaviors you wish to instill in your puppy.

These can be things like "heel," "sit," or "come." Ensure that everyone who lives with you knows about these commands and uses them. Also, you can use a hand gesture together with the command to help ensure that your puppy doesn't become confused. I once adopted a puppy and failed to keep my roommate engaged in the process of training, only to find out that we were using different words when asking the puppy to relieve herself. This ended with her looking up at us both in a confused way until we realized what was going on. Consistency in your commands will help your pet follow your orders happily and easily.

End on a positive note. When the puppy has a difficult time learning a new word or command you're trying to teach, end your training session by giving her a review of something she already knows. When she succeeds with this, remember to give her lots of praise. Keep in mind that if the puppy becomes frustrated or bored, it won't be productive for learning. Sticking with a command when your puppy has clearly lost interest or can't seem to follow it is counterproductive.

React quickly. You need to respond with praise or treats immediately after your puppy has performed in the desired way. This must happen each and every time she reacts appropriately in a given situation. The goal is to have the puppy connect her behavior with praise or a treat. This means that you need to keep treats on hand at all times when you're first teaching your dog simple commands.

You can gradually phase out treats for training, using them sparingly, as soon as the puppy has figured out a specific behavior. There will eventually come a time when treats aren't needed, but rewards and praise should always be used whenever your puppy acts correctly or obeys you. Continue using positive methods and reinforcement for maintaining desired behavior in your pet. Training based on rewards and praise will allow you to create a wide range of good behaviors in the puppy, fostering mutual confidence and trust in each other.

Your Puppy's First Day at Home

Countless techniques exist for training your puppy, many of which use methods based on punishment or fear. These can be anything from acting intimidating with your puppy, pushing, poking, yelling, disturbing them with noises, tying them up, flicking them, and more. There is no shortage of punishment-based methods for puppy training, and the shared factor in these methods is that the dogs don't have a choice to follow through on a specific action to get a reward. The puppies, in these cases, respond only to pain, discomfort, or fear. In other words, they are trying to avoid an unpleasant outcome that they don't wish for.

What do these methods lead to?

Not responding or shutting down. Often, when you use techniques based on fear or punishment, your animal will simply stop responding to you, or shut down completely. This doesn't allow the dog to learn new, favorable behaviors. Instead, it teaches them to fear the intimidator. Although you can get a pet to be obedient this way, it isn't as beneficial to you or the puppy.

The puppy freezing up. Many times, the animal stops doing anything at all, which can lead to the puppy suppressing her natural behaviors. Unfortunately, some people think of a still animal as an obedient or good dog, rather than a fearful dog. When a dog becomes still after being subjected to fear-based training techniques, they are showing that they are afraid.

This is not the basis of a healthy relationship with your pet. Doesn't the idea of your dog willingly obeying you, and being happy while doing it, sound better? This is what positive reinforcement puppy training is all about. The choice of how you will train your new companion is entirely yours. Your puppy, the one learning in this case, has no say in how you will teach him new skills. Science has proven that there are plenty of side effects to using punishment-based techniques for learning, such as heightened anxiety, escape or avoidance of the teacher, aggression, or fear. Your puppy may even become afraid of anything associated with his punishment, such as the room you punished him in.

Why Positive Reinforcement Works for Puppy Training

There is no reason training must be based around punishment or cruelty. Using positive methods leads to a well-trained dog that is happy to listen to you. Here are some other benefits to utilizing this method:

An enjoyable bond. It's true that most pet owners don't encounter dire situations resulting from the methods used for their puppy's training, but most of us wish for a companion who is fun to live with, and who also enjoys being around us. Life with your pet is much more enjoyable when you don't have to bully them into following your commands.

Low stress. One major benefit to using positive reinforcement is it creates a lower stress threshold within the home. This builds a relationship with your dog centered on low stress, cooperation, trust, and pleasant encounters with each other.

An obedient pet. The care and respect that results from using this method for training comes back to you tenfold. Your puppy wishes to spend more time with you, acts in desirable ways more often, and likes following your commands.

Puppy training can be hard, and a balance must be found between instinct and incentive, along with rewards and expectations. Positive reinforcement training is growing more and more in popularity and it's for a good and simple reason. Puppies learn positive behavior when given incentives for performing well. Punishment is not necessary for this, in the form of physical actions or harsh reprimands. Here are some considerations to think about, before starting your training process:

What do you want out of this? You can begin by asking yourself exactly what you hope for your puppy to learn from you. As a good trainer, you must think about the environment and the motivational factors for your dog, along with your own expectations and goals around this process.

Stay involved and be consistent. The more time you spend with your new companion, the better this will go. Success is entirely up to you. There are only a few reasons you end up with a disobedient dog, and these are a lack of focus and interest from the human, the trainer being inconsistent, or using training methods you don't like.

The most important thing to remember is that your dog is not an object that needs fixing. This is a friend and companion you will hopefully have for many years. The training process is as much for your dog's happiness as it is for yours. Let's begin with the first day you bring your new companion home.

The Puppy's First Day at your Home

This is an exciting and fun time for most pet owners. Some find it to be simple and easy, while others find it rather sleepless. Here are some key points to keep in mind to make your first night a smooth one:

A calm and quiet environment. When you adopt a young puppy, until it has come home with you, it's been with its siblings and mother in a familiar place. It's recommended that the dog's first seven days at your house should be calm and quiet, allowing the puppy to meet the new family and explore its new home. You might be excited about showing your new friend off to your friends, but there will be plenty of time for this later.

Teach the dog his or her name. You should first begin by allowing the puppy to become familiar with his or her name. This shouldn't take long to achieve. Start calling your dog by the chosen name right away, and make sure you use it a lot.

Allow the Puppy to Know the Proper Relieving Area

Next, introduce the puppy to the area that you have designated for it to relieve itself. For me, this was the grassy area out behind the house.

Use a leash. Bring your puppy outdoors with a leash on. When your dog is small, a shorter leash is okay, but an extendable leash might be better as he or she grows up.

Give a command. Next, think of what you want to have as your command for the puppy to relieve himself. This can be "go potty" or whatever else you choose. Keep in mind that your dog may have never heard these words before.

Give him time. Now, let your dog have some time to empty his bladder or bowels. If 15 minutes go by and he still hasn't gone, you can bring him back inside and try in another 10 minutes.

Praise the correct action. When your dog finally goes, make sure you praise him, but only if he went to the designated area. After this, allow him to explore your home (supervised and always within your sight). Continue to talk to your dog, using his name, to make him feel comfortable and at home.

Keep in mind that puppies piddle very often, due to their tiny bladder capacity. You should expect your dog to need to go at least once every two hours or so. You need to keep your eye on him at all times when he is inside. It's to be expected that your puppy has accidents here and there, because he is just learning the right habits, and he has such a small bladder. This is a basic introduction to what it means to potty train your dog, but we will go into deeper detail about this in chapter eight of this book.

If it doesn't Go Well at First. If he didn't go in the proper area, never shout at or punish him for this. This teaches your dog to have a negative association with a natural bodily function, and will only heighten the risk of your dog hiding behind your sofa to relieve himself.

Your Puppy's Sleeping Quarters

If you have ever raised a puppy, you already know that this is when it might get a little stressful. Many puppy owners realize that when they bring their dog home for their first overnight stay, sleep is not going to happen. The puppy will probably feel lonely at night, and let you know in a very vocal manner. Here is how to make your puppy feel less lonely and more comfortable:

Small sleeping quarters. The place your puppy sleeps, at first, should be a small comfortable bed. This should be in an area free of drafts, in your room, preferably near your bed. Eventually, your dog won't need this, but it's needed at first, so the dog doesn't get up to mischief in the night, or turn the entire house into his relieving area. I once made the mistake of allowing my puppy free roam in the house on her first night, and woke up in the morning to find an embroidered pillow my grandmother had made me in shreds on the living room floor. Trust me on this!

Crying at night. If your puppy cries at night, which is quite likely during the first few weeks, bring him outdoors to his designated relieving spot, on a leash. After he has relieved himself, he goes back into the bed. At night, no play time or treats are necessary; simply place him back in the bed so he knows to fall asleep again.

Don't let your puppy sleep with you. This can be a hard one, considering how cute your new friend is, but don't let your dog go to sleep with you, as it will encourage an undesired habit to form. This can be hard when your puppy is crying in the night, but you must leave her in the bed to teach her positive habits and know that crying won't achieve anything.

Get her a stuffed animal. You may find it helpful to get your dog a stuffed toy that she can sleep and snuggle with at night. You can buy this before adopting the dog, and leave it at the breeder's to get the scent of her littermates on it, so the puppy can feel at home and smell this familiar scent at night.

Each and Every Dog is Different

Always remember that each dog in this world is different, even dogs who are the same breed. Some find that the initial weeks of puppy training can be difficult, but it's all for a good cause. You may find that the hardest part of this is at night. Some puppies simply refuse to come around to their bed. They may bark, cry, howl, and whine, keeping you from a restful night.

Using praise at nighttime. In the first three or four weeks, you might have a hard time sleeping through the night with your new puppy, but make sure you stay firm about the bed. You might find it useful to help your dog get to sleep by telling them that they are a good dog, and by just talking to them for a few minutes when they aren't crying. If they start again, you simply remain silent until they stop. To try to get the puppy to be quiet, you can softly encourage them by saying "hush," or "quiet now."

Remember that this is about reinforcing positive behavior, not punishing negative behavior. Your dog will soon get the picture and realize that being calm and quiet at night is favored over making lots of noise.

Consistency and patience: During these initial stages, consistency and patience are your best friends. Within a few weeks of staying consistent about leaving your dog in her own bed at night (with bathroom breaks, of course), and giving her praise when she is good and quiet, she will stop keeping you up in the night. Eventually, you will have a well-behaved dog as a result of this consistency.

Training Foundations

To begin your training journey, you should get started off right. Your dog must know exactly what you expect her to do, which will allow her to feel comfortable with her ability to do what you want. Training puppies is all about reward and correction. Corrections for your puppy should:

Never be physical. This is highly important; you should never be angry or harsh toward your pet. When you must correct undesirable behavior in your puppy, hurting or spanking is out of the question, and will only set you back.

Be firm and respectful. When correcting your dog, all that is needed is a respectful, firm "no." You don't need to use a harsh tone or even raise your voice to get the message across. In fact, simply using a stern, serious voice will notify your puppy she is in the wrong.

The Right Way to Use Praise with your Puppy

Praise should be used often when training your new furry companion. It costs you nothing and shows that you approve of how your dog is acting. Another form of positive reinforcement is using dog treats. Treats are very helpful when it comes to first training your dog, although it can be hard to know how to do this right. You may find it tempting to give them out too often, but the key here is to be balanced in your approach.

Rewards are something your dog enjoys. Rewards, when used in training, are simply a response from you that your dog enjoys. This can be verbal praise, affection, a dog toy, or treats. We will go into more detail on how to use treats effectively in the next chapter of this book.

Use the proper tone. Your dog must learn to enjoy being praised. If you get into the habit of giving your dog a small treat while praising him or her with a positive and happy tone, they will come to realize that praise is a reward on its own, even without the added treat.

Treats should be small. Use small treats for your dog, about pea sized. Try to use them sparingly, especially in creating a positive association with praise, and for when they obey commands. Always use verbal praise in combination with treats.

Dog Training Tools

Dogs are considered man's best friend, and we love and admire them for being friendly and loyal. As such, we should give them the right care and the protection they need, since we already consider them as a member of the family. In this regard, a dog training lesson would be helpful for your pet pal to learn essential skills, fix bad habits, and take control of his behavior, as well as educate him with life-saving obedience commands.

Some people think that training a dog is a complex task, while still others believe that some dogs are not trainable. The truth about this is, with the right approach and dog training tools, all dogs can be trained – and it can be easy and fun. Interested in training your four-legged buddy? You may need to take a look at these dog training tools first.

Clickers

The clicker training tool provides an efficient means of communication between the dog and his human trainer. For dogs, click means treat. Practicing the mechanics of this tool helps deliver a clear message so that the dog trainee will understand the essential command in the click. You can practice using this tool even without your dog, or before you use it together, so you can be comfortable with it.

Tranquility Supplements

Dogs might feel anxious or nervous during the training session. A tranquility or calming supplement is an herbal formula that helps control and balance your dog's nervous system to avoid the uncharacteristic behavior. It is designed specifically for animals to relax the mind and stabilize emotions and nerves.

Housetraining Tools

Housetraining tools are various items your dog can use while training at home. They would include a training pad, potty patch, wrap, cover-ups, dog litter, and diapers. Teaching your dog the house's daily routine is one of the most important skills he needs to learn. Just make sure the surroundings are safe and free from harmful objects.

Dog Training Bags

These are multi-purpose dog training pouches or organizers designed to store all the necessary training tools and treats and keep them close to hand. It has a roomy compartment and also features a magnetic closure, inside or side pocket, waste bag dispenser, zippered compartment, belt clip and belt loops and D-ring attachment.

Target Sticks

Dog training instructors use target sticks to teach a dog to move to a particular place. It is very convenient and can easily be carried in a pocket or bag when needed. Using this stick, your dog can learn to follow the target as well as learn many tricks and skills.

Collars and Harnesses

his dog gear is essential for your dog's ultimate safety and can contribute to pleasant walks or a better travel experience for the owner. Choose a leash that you feel comfortable using, and gives you the best control on the walk with your dog.

Toys

Play is important with your puppy or young dog, and so is having an appropriate toy they can use and enjoy. A treat dispenser, chew toys, dog exercise aids, bicycle exercisers, comfort puppies, dog training toys, and tug toys are ideal toys that help to enhance your dog's body, mind, and familiarity with things.

Muzzles

A muzzle is sometimes recommended to ensure the safety of the trainers and keep a dog from causing injury, as some dogs become aggressive during training or when being handled by other people.

If you think it won't be ideal for you to train your dog on your own, you should consider getting the help of a professional dog trainer to address your dog's needs, as well as to make the dog training process easier for you.

Dog Training Techniques

Start with the Basic Commands

The simpler your command, the more motivated your pet will be to respond. Save those that are more complex for later. Begin with the basics: sit, heel, stay, and come. Once he has mastered these commands both on and off his leash, move on to more difficult ones. For instance, teach him to "drop it," "go to your place," and "look at me."

Always use positive reinforcement. Many owners assume they must either reward or punish their pets based on whether they respond correctly or incorrectly (respectively) to commands. Avoid punishing your dog. If he responds properly to your instructions, reward him with praise and a treat. If he fails to do so, withhold his reward. That alone is sufficient punishment and will motivate him to succeed.

Make the sessions enjoyable. You want your canine to look forward to the training sessions. First, keep them under ten minutes; short sessions will help you retain his interest. Second, end each session by giving him a command he has already mastered. This gives you an opportunity to end by praising him and giving him a treat. Your pet will look forward to the next time he can earn both.

Practice with distractions. Your dog may be able to respond easily to commands he knows well in the relative silence of your home. However, the outside environment might pose a few distractions. After he has mastered certain commands, practice outside where people are walking and cars are passing. Doing so trains your pet to ignore things that are occurring around him, and instead focus on you. This skill may one day become valuable if you need to get his attention quickly.

Shorten your commands. Brevity is important since your dog can easily become confused with longer commands. Whenever possible, use single words. For example, tell him to "sit" rather than "sit down." Tell him to "stay" rather than "stay right there." The shorter, the better.

Train him to be patient. Training your dog to "stay" for extended periods teaches him to control himself and remain patient. Begin by telling him to stay for 10 seconds while you stand nearby. Once he has done so several times in a row, increase the time to 20 seconds, and stand a few feet away. Continue to do this until he can remain calmly in his spot for 60 seconds while you stand 10 or 15 feet away from him. Also, establish a word that releases him from his spot (e.g., "Done!"), so he'll know when he has responded correctly.

Provide his reward quickly. Your dog must be able to recognize that the reward she is receiving (a treat, praise, etc.) is due to a particular behavior. If you wait too long, she may fail to associate one with the other. Provide praise and treats within a second of her correct response. This helps ensure she'll connect her actions with the rewards, and respond correctly in the future.

Training your dog is essential to helping her become a better companion for you and your family. It's the only way she'll know how to please you. Even if you enroll her into professional obedience classes, take additional time to train at home.

Nutrition for Your Dog

It is said that the way to a man's heart is through his stomach. We love to eat, and woe betide anyone who dares get in the way of good food. At the end of the day, however, good food isn't just something exploratory for the senses, it is also a way for us to keep ourselves healthy. Nutrition, in fact, is high on the list of what keeps us healthy and what gives us the strength and capability to stay on top of our health.

For our dogs, nutrition is also important. Just as with humans, dogs need the right nutrition to keep them going. Food provides important fuel to keep your dog active, and it also ensures that he doesn't find it difficult to go about his daily activities. The problem with humans when it comes to food for their dogs is that they often forget that their dogs need a canine diet, and although they may treat and love their dogs like humans, they have specific needs when it comes to their nutrition.

Dog Food Choices

Our dogs are our special friends, our companions. They rely on us to provide them with a loving home where they can feel safe, and they can get the best care we can afford. To do this, we need to feed them good food.

There are many opinions about dog food, what is good and what is bad. The media often provides us with huge amounts of advertising regarding just what is best for our pets. However, do they really have our dogs as a top priority, or do they have their bottom line as their priority? You decide after this brief review.

I believe we most often find ourselves at the supermarket, realize we need dog food, look for a name brand commercial food, check the price or see what is on sale, grab a bag and take it home. I have found that I have read the advertising on the label like 'nutritious', 'top quality,' 'high protein,' 'high energy,' or any other leading slogan, and those catch my eye. I feel that I am purchasing something good for my dog, and I don't take the time to read the ingredients because I assume the slogans wouldn't lie. I feel I am an educated shopper because I have seen the ads in magazines or on TV. Most of the time, however, these supermarket specials are not the high quality dog food we are led to believe, and we should take the time to understand just what the ingredients really are.

In my research, I have discovered what some of the terms in the ingredients actually mean. On the surface, they sound good; however, they are not as good as we think they are. Here are a few of the most common and important ingredients that we need to be aware of when purchasing good quality dog food.

Meat or poultry. These sound good, but ask yourself, "What *kind* of meat or poultry?" Meat and poultry are general terms, so you really don't know what is in the dog food. Is it beef, lamb, pork, chicken, turkey, goose, duck, or some other animal? Is this ingredient human grade, or leftovers from some processing source? The meat source is unknown.

Meal. Meat meal or poultry meal still does not specify the protein source. 'Meal' means the water has been removed so you get a more condensed product, but the animal is not specified, and is the animal source palatable for our pets? If it says 'chicken meal,' 'turkey meal,' or some other specific animal meal, that is good quality.

Rendered meat. This can be any meat from animals that are dead, diseased, dying, or disabled. The animals may have had some medicines or chemicals in them before they were processed. Our pets should not eat these.

By-products. This term is misleading because you don't know what the by-products are from. It could be hoofs, beaks, ears, etc. It is unknown. Not too appetizing!

Grains. Grains are often fillers and they do not have good protein value for our dogs. Our pets need more meat, such as beef, chicken, turkey, salmon, etc. Grains like corn, wheat, corn gluten, or wheat gluten are not good for dogs because dogs can be allergic to these grains. Other grains, such as oats or barley, are okay. The grains, however, should not be listed within the top four or five ingredients.

Animal fat. Again, from which animal? From fish and chips? Skimmed off of the top of a processing source? Dogs need fat, and chicken fat is good.

Brewer's yeast. Brewer's yeast is a good ingredient, but don't get it confused with brewer's rice. They are two different things, and brewer's rice is not very nutritious.

Preservatives. What kind of preservatives? BHA and BHT are often linked to cancer. Vitamin C and vitamin E are good preservatives.

You can do further research and make your own decisions. I was in a nationally known pet store recently, and they had several well-known commercial (low quality) pet foods that you would see at your supermarket, so don't be fooled. Read the ingredients.

Remember also that puppy food is often quite different from adult dog food, and puppies and dogs should not usually be fed the same food. They have different needs.

If you decide to change your dog's diet, do it over a period of 7-10 days so it doesn't upset his system. Slowly introduce his new food in small quantities, mixed in with his current diet at first. Increase the new food every couple of days, and decrease his current food until you have made the switch completely.

Dry dog food is the most convenient way to feed your dog, and always have plenty of water available for him to drink. Using a combination of dry and canned food is a very acceptable choice, and you don't need to use the same brand for both. As long as you feel you are selecting good quality food and your dog likes the flavor, you have made a great decision! Changing occasionally to another high quality food for variety is also a good choice.

If you find a dog food that has human grade ingredients, you have found a quality product. Don't be afraid to check out the manufacturer on their website. The price tag may be more, but you will have a healthier dog and fewer visits to the vet. Also, a dog eating a high quality dog food will not have a desire to eat as much, so you will save there. Your dog will have more energy, be healthier, and have a more beautiful, shiny coat.

Making your Puppy's Food

Pets can suffer from some of the same ailments and diseases as humans, so it would stand to reason that to offer your pet the best possible healthy lifestyle, it's advisable to make available the most nutritious food options you can. The nutritional value of some dog foods is low due to high amounts of fillers such as grains, corn, and soy products. Dog food producers use these fillers because they're cheap and allow them to stretch out the meat ingredients over more volume. Besides the fact that your pet is getting less meat, these fillers can cause an allergic reaction with your pet, and over time, sensitivities can build up causing a whole host of health-related issues.

To safeguard your dog from the health risks associated with consuming processed commercial pet food, many pet owners have taken to creating home-cooked food for their pets. Since you're in control of what you put into your pet's food, quality in equals quality out! It's simple to do, and the benefits to both you and your pet are amazing.

The main reason many pet owners choose to make their own food is freshness. Those commercially prepared foods sitting on the grocery shelf can be there for months and months, and then come home to sit in your pantry for even longer until they're consumed. When you make your food, it's as fresh as it gets.

Another benefit when making your own pet food is that you don't have to worry about recall notices about contaminated products in commercially produced products. Those are all too common, and as a responsible pet owner, you have to be vigilant about keeping an eye out for recalls. It's a constant worry, and if you don't catch the notice in time, you can unknowingly serve your pet food that will make her ill. This can lead to expensive vet bills and added worry and stress to you as an owner.

Some pets have diagnosed illnesses that require constant monitoring. Diabetes is one of those illnesses that can be controlled by diet; however, doing this using commercially prepared food is not an option. By controlling the exact ingredients and the amounts, you can tailor your pet's food to suit whatever restrictions may be needed to improve and stabilize your pet's health.

Another benefit of feeding your pet homemade food is the extension of their life. Studies released have shown that animals who consume a diet full of high quality nutritious homemade food outlive other animals by up to eight years. They are better able to ward off diseases and conditions that afflict commercially fed pets, and thus outlive them. A pet fed homemade food has all of her nutritional requirements met, and therefore enjoys an abundance of energy and can participate in an active, healthy lifestyle.

Researching expertly created homemade pet food recipes and creating your own meals is an investment in your pet's future. As a pet owner, and almost assuredly an animal lover, you can only want the best possible life your pet, and the small amount of time spent preparing meals is a small price to pay to help ensure your pet is afforded that life.

Puppy Potty Training

Puppy potty training is easier than you think. Unfortunately, one common reason people give their dogs away is because of their inability to get their dog to stop pooping and peeing on the carpet.

Before you give your puppy or dog away, try these five simple rules of puppy potty training that will make your life (and your dog's life) easier – and your house cleaner.

Rule 1: Watch.
When you bring your puppy home, always keep one eye on the dog at all times and the other eye on whatever other task you may be involved with. If you cannot keep your eye on your pup at all times, then you must confine him to a crate. Why?

Rule 2: Crate.
How does keeping your puppy in a crate stop him from peeing and pooping on your carpet, floor, or bed? First of all, the reason the dog pees and poops in your house is because he is comfortable doing so. You have to make the experience of peeing and pooping in the house very unpleasant. Every single time your dog pees and poops in your house – be it accidentally or purposefully – you must give him an immediate strong correction. You have to be able to correct your puppy as soon as he urinates or defecates in your house. If you're not constantly watching him, or if you do not have him confined to one area, you will not catch him in the act, nor will you be able to correct his behavior.

The crate acts as a deterrent from pooping in the house because your dog sees his crate as a sanctuary, so he will wait to eliminate until you take him outside.

Dogs don't like to lie in their poop, and the crate must only be big enough for the dog to stand, sit, and lie comfortably. If she poops in there, she won't enjoy the experience.

Never give your dog free reign of your home until your dog is 100% house proofed.

Rule 3: Have a spot.
The third rule of puppy potty training is that you should take your dog to eliminate in the same spot all the time. As soon as you see your dog getting

ready to eliminate, quickly grab him up and take him outside to the predetermined spot.

When you get there, give the command. What's the command? Whatever you want it to be. "Get busy" is a good one.

Lavish praise is a must. Immediately after your puppy eliminates in the predetermined spot, give him lavish praise. It is essential that you praise your dog when he behaves in a way that pleases you.

Dogs are creatures of habit. By taking your dog to the same place to eliminate all the time, he will then associate that spot with the correct place to eliminate. He will also expect praise for it.

Associating a command with his elimination also means that you can take him anywhere and give him the command to "get busy" and he will go wherever you want him to go.

Rule 4: Eliminate the odor.
Puppy potty training Rule 4 is to buy an odor eliminator. Your dog's urine will stay in your carpet if you use regular soap and water or some other normal detergent.

Once your dog has marked his spot, he will continually go to eliminate in that spot. So that means you need to use an agent that completely removes and neutralizes the odor.

Rule 5: Have a routine.
Last, but not least, get your dog on a very strict and consistent feeding and drinking schedule. You must feed and water your dog at the same time every single day. Doing so will make your dog have to go to the bathroom at the same time every day.

For some dogs, this means right after his meal. Other dogs may take longer. The trick is to watch your dog and time him after each meal. Then you'll be able to anticipate when he wants to do his business.

If you don't feed your dog on a consistent schedule, you'll never know when he has to go to the bathroom, which is frustrating for you, because your house will smell of poop, and frustrating for your dog, because he will get corrective measures, which will be unpleasant for him.

A small caution about unlimited and free access to water – unless your dog is 100% housebroken, I highly discourage you from giving your dog free and unlimited access to water.

Another key to potty training your puppy is to give your home a "den" like atmosphere. A puppy's natural instincts tell him that he can just relieve himself whenever and wherever – except for their den. The "den" doesn't have to start off as the whole house and usually can't be because it's too large. It can start off by designating a small, closed off area in your house as their den and put the puppy's crate in there. (You will probably need some kind of gate to hold your puppy in.) This designated area should be where your puppy sleeps and eats, which will tell him that is his den.

Your puppy may not like to relieve himself in his den, but he will if he has to. For the first few months, you will have to take your puppy outside after he plays, eats, and gets up from a nap (these are the most common times when puppies will relieve themselves). Plan to take him out every 30-45 minutes.

For the first three months of your puppy's life, he will only be able to hold his bladder for about seven hours during the night. You can extend this time to about nine hours by putting your puppy to bed for the night and getting him up at about the same time every day. This consistency will keep your dog from waking up at late hours in the night and relieving himself. The first thing you should do when getting him up is carry him outside. If you let him walk, he will likely go potty.

By following these five puppy potty training rules and other tips, you'll be able to housetrain your dog in as little as 10-14 days.

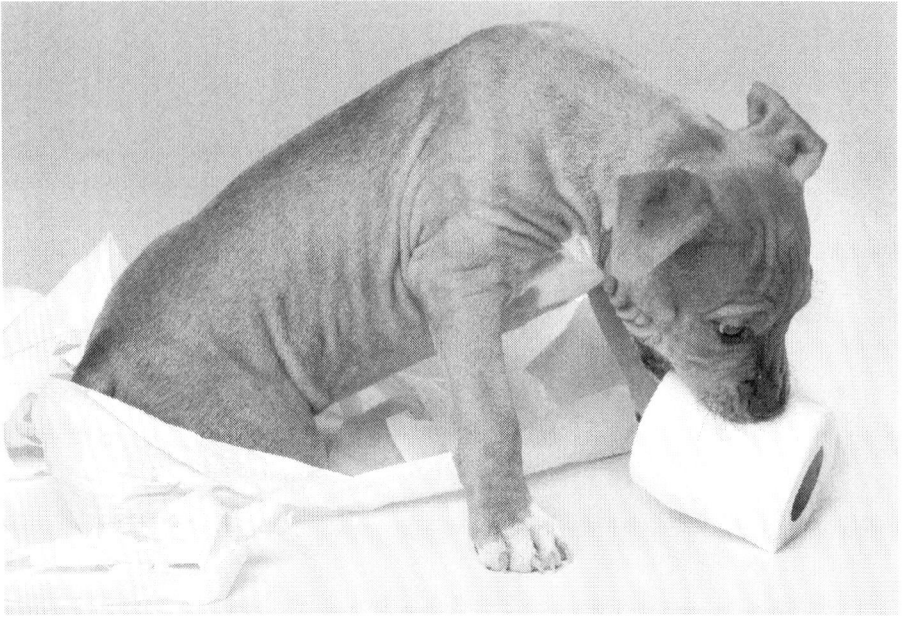

Clicker Dog Training

Exactly what is "clicker dog training"? Why should anyone care?

First, the concept of clicker training is simple. You're incorporating this dog training technique to teach your dog to relate the clicker sound – an intense, sharp sound that your dog will perceive at a distance of 20+ yards – with a particular command that you provide. The purpose of this process is to get your dog to do something specific, and subsequently reward that behavior with the clicker sound.

Okay, I can surely recognize your position that this technique may take a little longer than a shock collar. However, we love our dogs and don't want to inflict pain on them. From this perspective, clicker dog training is humane and may be utilized for much more than dog barking issues. Moreover, have you thought about this? Clicker dog training is inexpensive! And there are no safety issues.

This training technique will not begin with the use of a clicker. It will be necessary for you to view the clicker as a response to your dog's good conduct. One way in which to accomplish this is with a bag of treats. You can purchase a clicker for approximately $2 from a nearby pet store.

At the beginning of training your dog to respond to a clicker, remember these three steps: first, clearly establish the conduct you desire (i.e., your dog is to do something you choose). The behavior you seek may be sitting, speaking, rolling over, or something like that. Second, mark the correct response with the clicker, and third, give a reward.

Repeat this process on multiple occasions. Doing so will continue to reinforce the conduct as much as possible. Do not feel compelled to use treats every time. You will find that praise and petting will be equally effective.

After your dog has mastered the behavior, you will find that the clicker will easily permit transition to a verbal command you can use at any time, even when you do not have a clicker available. On those occasions when you intend to use the clicker, you'll now vocalize the command and click. Provide the reward upon successful performance of the desired behavior. Your dog will be able to associate all three activities rapidly.

Once you have mastered clicker dog training, your dog will respond to a vocal cue that is coupled with praise. You will find that your dog will simply learn it.

33

Once your dog realizes that the response pleases you, you will no longer need to use either treats or praise.

Clicker dog training has numerous situations in which it may be utilized. The incorporation of this form of dog training to control everything from a dog barking to aggressive behavior will make training your dog much easier. When you utilize a simple, sharp command, you will be able to mark and reinforce virtually any conduct you wish to modify!

Effective Dog Grooming Tips

One of the essential benefits of dog grooming is the way it stimulates the blood supply in your pet's skin. This is, of course, the reason why groomed dogs have healthier, shinier coats than other dogs. Here are some things you can do to care for your pet's grooming needs.

1. Brush the coat.
Brush your dog's coat every day to remove dirt and dust. Brushing enhances the distribution of natural oil all over the entire coat of your canine friend. It also helps to sort out tangled hair, protects the skin from irritation, and keeps dirt and ticks away.

Grooming is not meant for adult dogs alone. The best way to introduce your pet to grooming sessions is when she is still a puppy. This gets your pet used to being groomed, and she will surely love it, because she can have all of your attention and praise for a little while.

2. Trims the nails.
Nail trimming isn't just an ordinary part of the grooming routine. It is an important element of your pet's overall health and well-being. Allowing the nails to overgrow will give them a chance to break. Overgrown nails that are broken can cause your dog pain and soreness. It causes difficulty in walking, and sometimes arthritis.

Trim your dog's nails with a sharp dog nail clipper. Be sure to do it carefully, as you might cut a blood vessel by accident. You might also need a small bottle of blood-clotting powder to prevent bleeding just in case the unexpected happens.

3. Clean the ears.
When you are grooming your dog, you should include the cleaning of its ears as part of the normal routine. Your pet's ears need cleaning and proper care because they can easily get infected, especially when ticks and soil are allowed to stay there for a long time. You can cleanse your pet's ears twice a month.

When cleaning the ears, you should watch out for signs of infection so you can prevent it from getting worse. Other signs of dog ear infections include frequent scratching of the ears, frequent shaking of the head, and the presence of an unusual odor near or in your dog's ear.

The dog's inner ear color is an indication of its health. You will know that your pet is very healthy if its inner ears are pinkish in color.

4. Brush the teeth.

Like humans, dogs can get cavities if their teeth are not properly taken care of. Brush your pet's teeth with a baby toothbrush and pet toothpaste at least two times a week. You can ask your vet to show you how to brush your pet's teeth if you don't know how to do it.

5. Bathe the entire body.

Bathing is the main part of dog grooming. Before you start, you need to brush your pet's hair lightly. This will help to sort out tangles which are difficult to remove when the hair is wet. Tangles will become mats which are favorite spots of yeasts and bacteria.

Once you are done with brushing, you can now proceed to bathe your dog with water and mild pet shampoo.

Having a dog requires you to be sensitive and responsive to its basic needs. Your pet can be content with your attention and feeding, but he will become healthier, cleaner, and better looking if you groom him regularly. Dogs love to be groomed. It's the time that they can have their master's undivided attention and love. It can help to keep them calm and assured of a great companionship.

Dog Housetraining

Everyone with puppies and dogs should know that it can be a challenge to housetrain, but with these tips, canine owners can understand how to train effectively, efficiently, and with less frustration.

When you get a puppy, you think it is time for cuddles and snuggles and playtime. However, it is time to housetrain your puppy as soon as you can! Keep in mind that a puppy is never completely housetrained until he is six months old, but depending on the breed, he will pick up good habits quickly. Put him on a feeding schedule so that it will be easier for you remember when he needs to go out. Puppy house training websites say you should let him out immediately after he eats or drinks and take notice of his body language.

Housetraining an adult dog is more difficult than housetraining a puppy. As we suggested in Chapter 8, pick a potty spot for your dog, for instance by the tree outside. He will have to go potty in that location every time he goes, and he will learn he is supposed to go outside. Also, training your dog to go potty by giving a particular command is a very effective way of housetraining a grown dog.

Remember that since your dog is an adult, he has old bad habits that are hard to break, so housetraining will take more time than if he was a puppy. Remember he wants to please you. Be patient with your dog; do not get frustrated with him if he has accidents in the house. Dog trainers say do not discipline your dog, but instead, use praise when he does something good.

As with puppies, grown dogs need their food and water monitored, and to be let outside afterward. If you have a male, consider having him neutered; it is almost irresistible for a male dog to make his mark.

Dog training is somewhat more difficult, but you can follow the same steps and procedures you would with a puppy. It might take a little longer. Work with her outside, and have her focus on you and work to ignore distractions like other animals and people. Clickers can be helpful with older dogs, too.

Remember to spend time with your dog, and learn to communicate the best you can. You'll still always reward a correct action. Even though your new pal cannot talk, she watches your body language and is very sensitive to emotions.

A common misconception is that dog obedience training is just for the ones who misbehave, but the truth is that all dogs could use a little obedience training. Their owners could, too! Dog obedience training is typically in a group setting, so it's harder – all the noises, animals, and people around are distracting. Be sure to use your clicker to keep her attention!

Some grown dogs have had many years without this kind of education. If the dog obedience training does not seem to work, or if your dog is uncomfortable in this setting, you can always try dog behavior counseling. Do your research first! You will need to find a certified trainer, experienced with insecure, anxious, inattentive, or fearful dogs.

Dog behavior counseling requires you to let your dog do things he is comfortable with, so do not push your dog or get frustrated with him. Always do your research before signing on for any training or counseling. You will need to find a method that works for both you and your dog.

Does Your Dog Need Obedience Training?

Not too long ago, it was a given that the only way to properly train a dog was to essentially beat the dog into submission. It was thought that until the dog had been broken mentally, it would not be responsive to commands. Fortunately, this prehistoric thinking has been largely relegated to the past, but intelligent obedience training is still recommended for most dogs.

Anyone who owns a dog larger than they can comfortably pick up at need should provide obedience training. Smaller dogs can also benefit from training, but for dogs over 30 pounds, it should be considered a necessity. Large dogs in the range of 50 or more pounds can cause serious problems – either to people or other pets – if not trained properly.

Dogs have evolved from wild canines that live in a very structured society. Every wolf, coyote, or African hunting dog knows exactly where he or she stands in respect to the rest of the pack. This hierarchical structure keeps the group peaceful. As dogs have moved into human society, they have become part of a human pack and must learn their place in each household.

Without obedience training of some kind, most dogs will try to move to the alpha position in a home, taking over from the humans. The dog will protect the people, but it will also expect the humans to defer to it. This is a very undesirable situation that can lead to aggression, not only to the immediate human pack, but to other humans as well. This is a potentially explosive situation when the dog involved is a large, strong breed.

The point of modern obedience training is not to produce a robot, but to help a dog understand its place in the home society, and to produce confidence. When obedience training is done with patience, positive reinforcement, understanding, and consistency, it will strengthen the bond between master and dog, and result in a dog that will be able to go more places and will probably remain in the home for its lifetime. Most dogs that wind up in shelters do so because their owners are unable to control them; these dogs often exhibit aggression.

A dog can receive obedience training either at home or in class. Going to a class for obedience training can be a good choice to provide socialization with other dogs and people. Shy dogs can often get over their shyness by participating in a group. Regularly scheduled sessions will help make sure that training continues, too.

The best time to start training is while the puppy is young, although obedience training an adult dog is relatively easy, too. The keywords to successful obedience training are positive reinforcement and patience. Hitting a puppy or dog when an incorrect response is given will result in a dog that develops a fear of its owner. This dog is more likely to ignore commands in the future, and may become neurotic.

When using positive reinforcement for obedience training, you will be rewarding good behavior with treats and praise, and ignoring unwanted behavior. It does take longer for positive reinforcement training to take effect, but it is permanent, unlike training that has been conducted using fear and pain. Keep sessions short and if either you or the dog shows signs of boredom or aggravation, stop immediately and do something else.

The dog's breed will have some bearing on how well obedience training goes. Certain breeds such as Border Collies and Labrador Retrievers are very easy to train, while other breeds, such as Pekingese and Dalmatians are more difficult. Difficult breeds to train are not necessarily unintelligent; in most cases they are simply stubborn.

Small dogs are often the most difficult to obedience train for several reasons: they are often very stubborn, and they consider themselves to be above such things. When our French Bulldogs were puppies, we tried to give them some basic obedience training simply as a safety measure. All three pups learned the basics (come, sit, stay) almost immediately. Two or three repetitions were enough for them to master the commands. However, after they did master them, they all refused to do them anymore. If you told them to come, they would sit or lie down, and a command to stay resulted in them tearing towards you.

Small dogs do have a different outlook than many larger breeds, and if you do decide you want to add one of these companions to your household, it would be best to accept that despite the dog's intelligence, it can be untrainable in some cases.

Dog Barking Control

When people are searching for a way to socialize their dog by controlling their barking, they have a choice of barking control collars to choose from. These will usually fall into one of three groups. There are dog collars that offer bark control through the use of scent, others offer bark control by the use of sonic sound, and then some use electric shock. The method a dog owner will choose to use will depend on the temperament of the dog, and the beliefs of the dog owner.

For example, there are dog owners who feel that using a barking control collar based on scent is the best method to train their dogs. These bark collars are equipped with a canister of citronella oil. The cartridge is placed against the dog's throat, and it's activated by the movement of the neck when the dog barks. When the cartridge is set off, a spray of citronella oil will be released. This herbal oil isn't toxic, but it does have a very strong lemony scent. (This is the same oil that is used in bug repellant sprays.) The dog's nose is very sensitive, and they typically don't like the scent of citronella. This is why the spray of this scent makes a great bark control tool. When the dog barks, it will learn to associate the scent with its excessive barking. To avoid the spray of oil, the dog won't bark so much. Many dog owners feel that this is the most humane method of breaking a dog of its excessive barking.

Then there are sonic sound collars for barking control. The dog's barking also activates these. However, instead of emitting a blast of oil spray, this collar will send off a sharp sonic sound that only the dog will hear. The good news is that humans won't be bothered by this noise, but dogs will be irritated. Some dog owners don't like this method because they fear that this might hurt the eardrum of the dog. However, there are many safe brands on the market. The idea is to annoy the dog mildly, and not to harm him. In any case, this method has been shown to be effective.

Finally, there are the electric shock dog barking control collars. As the name implies, this collar gives the dog an electric shock when it barks. Needless to say, this method of bark control can be very controversial. But the humane dog owner should be aware of the fact that their dog will not be harmed using this method. The shock is the equivalent to getting a static cling shock. It will get the dog's attention, but it won't hurt the animal. This might be a great dog barking control collar for more aggressive dogs, or for dogs with severe and obsessive barking issues.

How to crate train your puppy

Crate training your puppy starts from the time you choose him from the litter, until you bring him home. This process continues for a couple more weeks after that.

Crate training for puppies three months or less

When you go visit your puppy from your breeder, bring an ample-sized box or container which will serve as his crate. You can choose to leave the crate at the breeder's place, or bring it along each time you visit. Either way, provide a piece of blanket or towel at the breeder's, so it will pick up the smell of the puppy's family.

If you've already chosen the puppy you want, ask the breeder if it's possible to have a temporary separation fence so you can spend time with the puppy without removing him entirely from his mother and littermates. Bring the crate inside this enclosure and try to get him acquainted with the scent. At this point, he may or may not enter the crate on his own. Don't rush this process. This can take anywhere between three days to a few weeks before he begins to trust the crate.

You can do this any time after the puppy has begun to open his eyes. Try to keep these sessions short – a couple of minutes at a time should be enough for the puppy to get acquainted with the crate.

Crate training for puppies three months and up

At three months old, your puppy should be ready to leave his family and become a part of yours. By now, he can walk and run (clumsily) and has started to become more curious about his surroundings.

Bring the crate inside the enclosure, but this time put the piece of cloth with his mother's scent inside the crate. This should pique his curiosity and make him want to enter the crate. There might be a few tentative attempts before he finally goes all the way in. When he does this on his own, give him a treat and praise him. Allow the puppy to come out and repeat the process again. This may take a few tries, as these sessions should only be a couple of minutes long.

You can also speed up the process by simply using a treat to get him to go inside the crate. Place a treat near his nose and then lead him towards the crate. Place the treat inside the crate and allow him to enter on his own to get to the treat. Once he is inside, give him another treat and praise him for a job well done. Entice him out with another treat, so you can repeat the process.

Once he is accustomed to the crate, it is time to start closing the door while he is inside. Just repeat the process of getting him inside with a treat and then reward him with some praise. Wait for him to calm down and then slowly close the door, while at the same time speaking kindly. After a few seconds open the door and let him out. Reward him with some treats and more praise for a job well done. Repeat this process over and over until he trusts the crate completely, even with the door closed.

Never ever slam the door on the puppy while crate training is going on.

The basics of getting your puppy in and out of the crate

The crate is going to be unfamiliar for your puppy and she may have some initial apprehension before she decides to enter it. You will need a lot of patience. This is the stage where you want to ensure that your puppy will see the crate as a safe place, and not as a cage.

So let's review the basics of how to get your puppy in and out of the crate without any hassles.

1) Bring the crate to the dog breeder's and place it near you when you're spending time with your puppy.

2) Play with her for a bit, and then lead her towards the crate. Never force the puppy into the crate. Use treats to engage her nose, and allow her natural curiosity to follow your hand (with the treat) into the crate. Allow her to come out again, or entice her with another treat.

Note: This process can take several attempts over the course of several visits. Again, you have to be very patient. The key here is to get your puppy accustomed to the presence of the crate. Getting in and out of the crate with ease is also part of the exercise to make your puppy feel safe with the crate around.

3) After your puppy is accustomed to the crate, it's time to practice closing the door while she is inside. Make sure that the puppy is in a relaxed state before

you close the door of the crate. Never close the door on an agitated or over-excited puppy, as this could become a negative experience for her, and may make her feel trapped inside the crate.

4) After several seconds, allow the puppy to get out of the crate. Repeat the process and once she is relaxed inside, make her stay inside the crate a little longer each time.

Note: once your puppy is extremely comfortable within the crate, you can now safely bring her home inside the crate.

As soon as you get home, simply lead the puppy out of the crate with treats. Give her lots of praise for coming out of the crate on her own.

Using the crate to acclimate your puppy to the new surroundings

You'll want to introduce your new puppy to your home to him bit by bit. Otherwise, your puppy is going to think he is free to go everywhere and do whatever he wants. Puppies who are allowed to do this often grow up to become destructive dogs. This is not something you want to happen. Let's follow the process for preventing it.

Removing your puppy from his familiar surroundings, and bringing him away from his mother and littermates, is going to stress him out. So let's use the crate to acclimatize him to his new surroundings

1. First, place the crate in the smallest room you have and leave your puppy alone for a couple of minutes. You can stay nearby where he can see or smell you, so he doesn't feel too anxious about being left alone.
2. After a couple of minutes, when your puppy is relaxed, allow him to come out on his own, or coax him with treats.
3. Allow him to explore the room a bit. He'll be curious about all the new things and he'll be sniffing around. You have to be vigilant and make sure you look for any telltale signs that he may want to poop or pee.
4. Once he gets used to that small room, you can introduce your puppy to an adjoining room. Allow him to go from one room to another and only place him back in his crate if he gets anxious. For the first few months, it's best to keep him to a certain area of the house. For instance, upstairs or downstairs could be off-limits.

5. As your puppy grows older, introduce more rooms, but always keep the crate readily available so he always has a safe place to go back to when he gets anxious.

Using the crate to stop your puppy from being homesick

Homesickness is a common issue with puppies who are separated from their mother and littermates. You'll know he misses his family if he starts whimpering or howling when he is left alone. Don't worry, this is normal and crate training can be used to address this issue.

1. Place the crate beside your bed. Make sure you can easily reach it without having to get out of bed.
2. Tap the top of the crate lightly when your puppy starts whimpering or making a sound. This should distract him, and snap him out of his current state of mind. Often, this will stop your puppy from making any noise.
3. Make sure you tap the crate immediately so that the puppy understands that you do not approve of the noise he is making. This will also assure him that you are nearby.
4. Over time, your puppy will become accustomed to his crate. His homesickness is going to fade, and you'll have a peaceful night. Make sure you give your puppy a reward for being quiet all throughout the night.

Note: you can also use a spray bottle that shoots a light jet of water to hasten this process. Simply spray your puppy when he starts whimpering at night. A light spray should remind him to quiet down.

Another thing you can do to comfort your puppy is to use the piece of cloth that has his mothers and siblings' scent on it in the crate. This should help ease the homesickness your puppy will experience during the first few days he is with you. You can also place a piece of cloth that has your scent in the crate as well, so your puppy will get accustomed to you quickly.

Using crate training as a socializing tool for puppies

Dogs are among the most social creatures in the animal world. They thrive well in many situations where there are interactions with people and other pets. But this does not come naturally, especially for puppies. Socialization can be intimidating to puppies. It is your responsibility to socialize your puppy properly and get him accustomed to the presence of other people and other pets without getting intimidated.

An improperly socialized animal can be a hassle in the future. You don't want your puppy to grow up into a fearful adult dog who will feel threatened around people or other animals.

You can use crate training to properly socialize your puppy so that you'll have a well-balanced dog in the future.

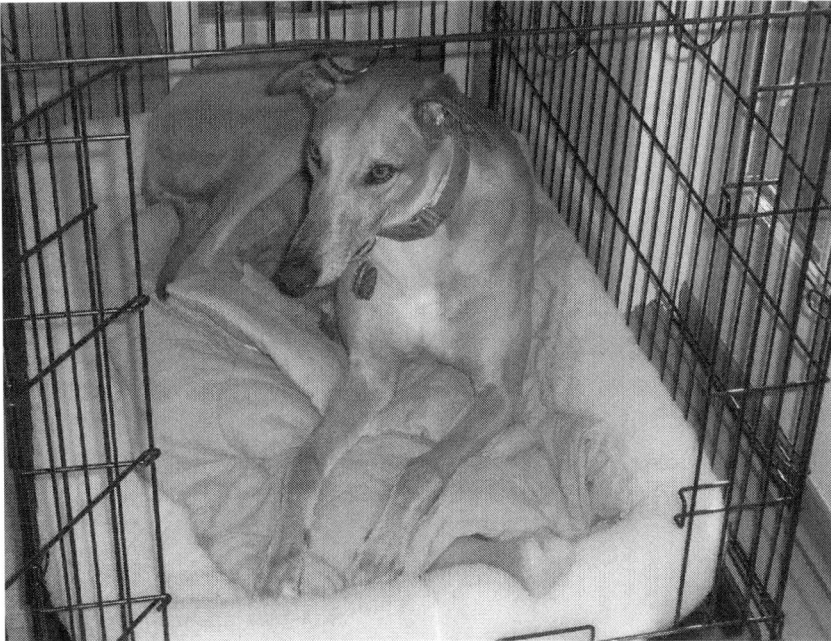

Socializing puppies to other people and family members

By now your puppy should be very comfortable staying inside his crate for extended periods of time, venturing out only to empty his bowels, eat or exercise. There should be no signs of anxiety. This is the right time to introduce your puppy to people and other pets.

1. Place the crate in an area that receives some traffic from people and other animals. Your puppy should be exposed to external stimuli, without being overloaded with the sights and sounds of the environment.
2. Get a family member in your household to accompany you into the room where the crate and the puppy are located. This will help your puppy identify the unique sound and smell this person possesses. This will also help your puppy realize that the person with you is not a threat and there is nothing to be afraid of.
3. Entice the puppy to get out of the crate and approach the other person so he can get used to the smell and presence of another human aside from you. Supervise the interaction between your puppy and that other person. At this point touching the puppy is not necessary. After a couple of minutes allow the puppy to climb back into his crate. Reward your puppy with treats.
4. Continue adding more people to interact with your puppy. Always make sure that you reward your puppy with praise and treats. Let the other people in your household give treats as well.

Socializing puppies to other household pets

Socializing your puppy with other animals in your household can be tricky. But if this is done properly, you'll have a more harmonious household.

Expose your puppy to other animals in the house while he's in his crate by placing his crate in an area frequented by other household pets. Do not force any interaction just yet, but allow the other pets to sniff around the crate. Reward both your pet and your puppy for good behavior.

Continue this type of interaction several times before letting your puppy out to have some physical contact with your other pet. Make sure you supervise the interaction at all times to ensure no one gets hurt.

After a couple of minutes, separate the puppy from the other pet and place him back inside the crate. Reward pets for good behavior if everything went smoothly.

Using crate training to make your puppy comfortable about traveling

Traveling is perhaps one of the most stressful events in any animal's life. Animals are used to moving around using their own feet. Traveling inside a vehicle can be quite disconcerting and suffocating for any animal at first, and it may take time for your pet to get accustomed to it.

You can use crate training to reduce the chances of your puppy getting stressed out during car trips or other forms of travel. Do this as early as possible so you won't have any issues when your puppy grows up.

1. Place the crate inside your vehicle and entice your puppy to climb into it using treats to engage his nose. Allow your puppy to climb in on his own. If he is too small, you might want to scoop him up and place him inside the car or provide

a ramp, but make sure he enters the crate on his own. This will take a lot of patience on your part.

2. Gently close the door to the crate once he is safely inside. Give your puppy some praise and rewards to get him into a calm and relaxed submissive state. Once your new puppy is relaxed enough, you can now close the door to your car and start the engine.

3. Short drives are ideal at first. Make sure you stop regularly to allow him to relieve himself or to stretch out every 30 minutes.

4. Once you've reached your intended destination, allow your puppy to come out of the crate by himself, by engaging his nose with a treat. Make sure you reward your puppy with praise or treats to make traveling a very positive experience for him! All of these things may seem like a hassle for now but once your puppy gets used to traveling you'll see that it was all worth the effort!

In short, crate training is a very important aspect in your puppy's development. It can address many issues in the future by instilling discipline at a very early age. Make sure you crate train your puppy to get a well-balanced dog in the future.

Things to Keep in Mind When Doing Dog Training

Dogs are beautiful, cute, and loving. They are a great pet and are quite rightly considered to be men's best friend. Well, there can be many problems if the dog is not trained properly. If you are training your dog all by yourself, then there are many things you should keep in mind, and some things you should *not* do when training your dog. Let's go over some of the do's and don't's.

1. Choose a suitable breed.
The most important aspect in dog training is that your dog must be suited to your personality. There is such a variety of breeds of dogs, and people tend to choose the good looking and cute ones. But you'll be spending a lot of time together, so you should be a good match. For instance, if you are an active person then you should own an active dog, or you'll get bored with him. Imagine the discomfort you'll feel, on the other hand, if you love to stay indoors watching TV, and your dog needs to be outside running around a lot.

Do research on the common traits of each breed you're considering. A mismatch in personality is the main reason for bad relations between the master and the dog.

2. Be patient and kind.
With dogs, accidents do happen, and you should not be violent or threaten them. Your dog has feelings, and it is important to have a trusting bond. Yelling and other harsh responses will not do you any good, and will affect your friendship with your dog. Scolding, yelling, or using a loud voice will make your dog afraid of you.

If something gets broken or spilled while your dog is moving around the house, you should be very calm, and you need to clean up the mess very quietly. The best thing to do at this moment is to take your dog outside and ensure some reward for doing something right, such as going potty outside. Again, patience and kindness are required in dog training.

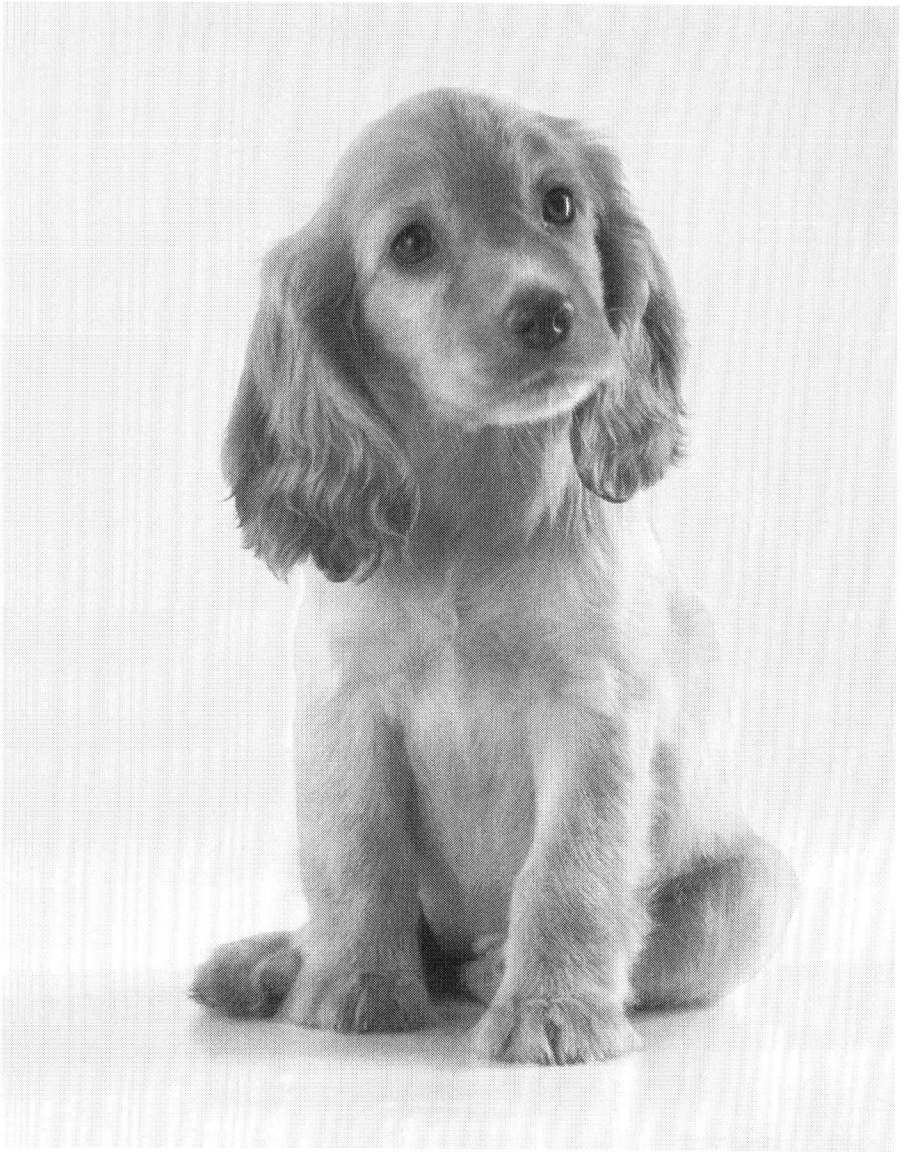

Treating Separation Anxiety in Dogs

Separation anxiety in dogs is a problem that many dog owners face. It can cause incessant whining, chewing, barking, and various forms of destruction to property. This leads a lot of concerned pet owners to search for answers as to how to treat and cure their dog of this problem.

Dogs are naturally inclined to be companions and loyal friends. They require your love and attention on a frequent basis. However, sometimes this love can cause consequences of an undesirable nature. If your dog becomes very attached to you, a problem can begin to arise when you to need to leave home. This is when the barking, whining, chewing, and destruction usually takes place.

The noise can be a great disturbance to neighbors and cause you to receive many complaints.

Many dogs and puppies get dog separation anxiety at some point in their lives. It is critical that this problem is addressed as quickly and as sensitively as possible. Once you notice that your dog is having these feelings, begin a step-by-step treatment plan immediately. It isn't an easy thing to cure, but once you can get to the cause, it becomes easier to fix. Try to see the problem from your dog's point of view. This will help you when you are going through the training process.

Dogs are social, and they want to be around their people for many reasons. If your dog had the choice, he would spend every second of his life with you. This is why it is common for your dog to experience drastic changes in behavior when you are absent from the home.

There are several ways to treat separation anxiety in dogs. Some say that medication is effective. However, this may not be a good idea since your dog could have an adverse reaction. Giving your dog some exercise before you go will help, in the sense that they will feel tired afterward and may want some time alone for a nap. Make a spot in your house that is just for your dog, such as a crate, to help him find independence. Or give him a comfortable mat or blanket next to his food and water bowls. Make this place as comfortable and cozy as possible, so he will want to spend time there.

It is not advisable to try "tough love" and ignore your dog, as this will only raise his anxiety level more. Separation anxiety in dogs can only be cured if the owner is loving and willing to get to the bottom of the problem.

The best cures for separation anxiety in dogs are consideration, compassion, and extra special care from the owner!

What You Need To Know About Dog Walking

Before you go for a walk, you'll need a leash. At the market you will find various kinds available. It's important to get a lead that that offers good control over your dog, especially when you are training a puppy. Retractable slip leads are very trendy these days. The slip lead is a single-piece lead with an O-ring at the end that is opposite to the handle. It will tighten around the dog if she pulls too hard. These slip leads are also known as British style lead, and they are often used in training or the show ring.

You will need to walk your dog regularly. According to experts, there are plenty of benefits that come with it, for both you and the dog.

Bond strengthening. Since you will be alone with your pet, you will have quality time together. Experts report that this time is important in forming a deep and trusting relationship with your dog. The time that you spend together with him also plays a vital role in his behavioral development, as you will know what habits he is developing, and can work to correct any bad ones.

Weight control. Just like humans, dogs are bound to gain plenty of weight when they lead a sedentary lifestyle. If you live in an apartment, your four-legged friend has little space to exercise; therefore, he gains weight. During the walk, he burns calories thus bringing about weight loss. And it'll do you some good, too!

Better mental well-being. If you exercise regularly, you can bear witness that you feel much better afterward. This is because your body discharges hormones that enhance your mental well-being. This is the same for your dog. When he exercises he feels better about himself, thus becoming a more relaxed companion.

More exposure. When you walk your dog, you expose him to new people, experiences, and settings. This helps him to learn new things which are crucial for growth.

Decrease loneliness. If you live alone, and work outside the house, this means your dog spends most of his time alone. Just like humans, dogs are social beings. When you are walking him, you give him company which helps him feel loved and valued.

Longer life. Since dogs who exercise are fitter and healthier, they tend to live longer. Since they have longer lives, you enjoy the company of your dog for a longer time.

Tips for walking your dog

While many people know that they need to walk their dogs, studies show that few dog owners know how to do it properly. To help you out, here are tips on how to properly walk him:

Always keep him on a leash. When your dog is on a leash you have full control of him, and you are the one in charge of the walk – not the dog. The best way to holding the leash is to wrap it around your hand so there is little space between you and him.

Treat him. It's always recommended that you train your dog during the walk. Some of the things you can work on are walking, sitting, and when to pull on the leash. When he behaves the way you want, you should reward him with his favorite treat.

Make the walk comfortable. Make sure the leash is made from a comfortable material, and that you apply gentle pressure. Remember the walk is meant to be fun. Also, the time of day that you walk him determines how comfortable the dog will be. For instance, you might avoid walking him at noon on hot days.

How to Make Your Puppy Stop Begging for Food

While having a puppy begging at the dinner table is virtually harmless, it can be quite an annoyance. It's a common problem, and the first thing you need to know to begin solving it is that begging is not an instinctual behavior. At some time during your puppy's life, you have trained him to do this, whether you know it or not.

It all starts when your puppy is hanging around the table during a meal. When someone slips the puppy a scrap under the table, or the puppy is fed leftovers afterward, the puppy will quickly learn to come back next time to wait and beg for more.

The number one way to stop the begging problem is to never let it start. This may seem obvious, but it only takes one instance of you feeding your puppy from the table to start a begging problem. A good rule of thumb I use is only to feed a puppy from his food bowl. This means that you can still feed your puppy scraps if you want to, as long as you are sure to put them in her food bowl first.

If you have been feeding your puppy scraps from the dinner table for a while now, then the begging can be difficult to stop. Luckily, there are a few different methods you can use to help.

First, stop feeding your puppy anything from the table. If possible, always have your puppy eat from her bowl.

As always with attention-seeking behaviors, when your puppy is begging you need to ignore her completely. Just pretend she is not there. After a certain period, any puppy will stop begging. Keep in mind that this method will probably not work overnight. If your puppy has been fed from the table for eight months, then it could take a month for your puppy to cease the begging.

One sure-fire way to stop begging is to put your puppy in her crate or in a different room during meal time. In this case, she will not have the opportunity to beg.

Another method is to feed your puppy during meal time, in hopes that she will be distracted enough by her meal to not bother you at yours.

Just remember that all in all you will just have to "out-stubborn" your puppy. Your puppy will persist in looking cute and begging for food. It is your job to stay strong and not give in in the hopes of your puppy one day not begging anymore.

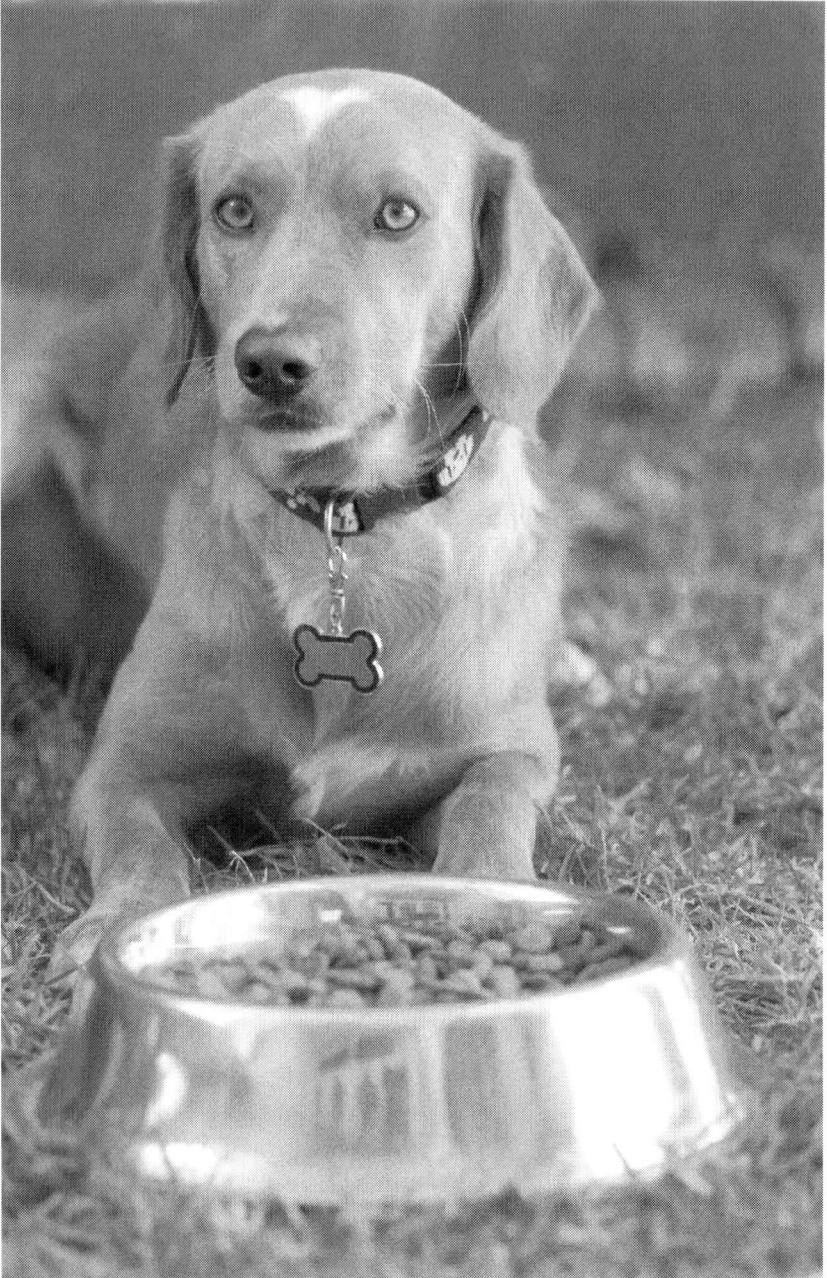

How to Fence Train a Puppy Quickly and Effectively

Installing an electric fence is one of the most effective methods of holding in your puppy. This can allow you to leave your puppy unsupervised for longer periods of time in the place he loves the most: the great outdoors. So what's the catch? The catch is that if you do not properly educate your puppy about the fence's boundaries and train him to come back into the yard when he is shocked, the fence is worse than useless.

The whole process of fence training usually takes around three weeks, with 15 minutes training time a day. This training consists of two main steps and then testing your puppy's progress at the end by adding distractions.

Disable the collar's corrective shock, so it will only beep. On some collars, there will be a switch. On other collars, you may have to manually disable it by covering the tongs in masking or electrical tape. Then introduce the fence by showing your puppy his boundaries, and teach him to jump back into the yard instead of out when he hears the beeping noise. This step consists mainly of positive reinforcement, so have your treats ready. This is to help prepare for when your puppy gets a shock one day, so he will not panic and jump out of the boundary.

Start off by putting your puppy on a leash and putting the disabled collar on him. Now, lead the puppy through the yard over to a boundary and let him cross the line. When you hear the beep from the collar, pull your puppy back into the yard and say "No, no, no," with a sense of urgency. After he is back in the yard, praise and treat him. Do this for 15 minutes a day for about a week, or until you notice your puppy start to come back in on his own after a beep.

Step two is almost the same as step one, but with a few changes. The main difference is that you are now adding the correction. Do this by either turning the shock back on with the switch, or removing whatever tape you used before to disable it. One thing to remember when turning on the shock is the level. Because this is the first time your puppy will experience the shock, you will not want the shock level to be too high. On the flip side, it cannot be too weak, or your puppy will not benefit at all from training.

Proceed as you did in step one – just lead your puppy to the boundary until you hear the beep. Then you pull the puppy back to the yard, treat, and praise. Keep in mind not to coddle the puppy too much after the shock. It is only static electricity, and it will surprise him more than hurt him. Also, if you make a big deal out of it, your puppy will too, which is not something you want. Do this step for the same 15 minutes a day for a week, or until the puppy refuses to cross the barrier.

The last part of the process of fence training is testing your puppy's training and making sure he is reliable to be left alone. You can do this by trying to lead your puppy over the fence with treats. If he refuses to follow, go back inside the barrier and give him the treat. Another way to test is to leave your puppy alone, off the leash in the yard. You can peek through the window to monitor him.

How to Train Any Puppy to Retrieve

Retrieving is a great way to use up your puppy's energy (and your own) and to strengthen the bond between you. Training your puppy to "go fetch" can be an easy process or a hard one; it all depends on your breed of dog. Some breeds, golden retrievers for example, are born with the natural instinct to retrieve and bring things back to you. You will still have to teach these types of dogs to drop the item, but overall it is immensely easier than trying to train other breeds of dogs, such as terriers, to retrieve.

One thing that almost all puppies have in common is that they love to chase, both you and their toys. We are going to use this fact to our advantage. As long as you have a long leash and a toy small enough for your puppy to pick up, you can do this fairly easily.

The first step in the getting your puppy to retrieve is to make him interested in the toy he is going to fetch. First, put his long leash on and command him to sit. Once your puppy is sitting, hold him back with one arm over his chest and wave the toy in front of his face. Continue to shake and wave the toy in front of your puppy until he is struggling to escape your one arm and get the toy.

When your puppy wants the toy quite badly, throw it a short distance from where you are and release the beast. When your puppy stands up to chase the toy, get up with him and trail behind a few feet. When your puppy grabs the toy, give the leash a slight pull (just enough to let him know to follow you) and run away back to where you started. He should chase or follow you back. This part will only work if you are high energy and upbeat the whole time, so be sure the puppy knows you're playing.

When you and your puppy have returned to where you started you need to make sure he does not run off with the toy. Do this by shortening the leash length to the point where your puppy is forced to stay within a foot or two of you. Now, the key is to make your puppy drop the toy without you having to fight or struggle for it. Be sure not to pull it out of his mouth. He will drop it on his own eventually, once he realizes you are not going to play tug of war. The game can only continue if he drops the toy, and he will eventually figure this out. The only time your puppy might not drop it is if he lies down to chew. In this case, you must try and coax him into letting go. Do this by lightly pulling on the toy. Every time he pulls back, let go – don't let the tug of war continue. Eventually, he will stop pulling back, and you can begin the retrieving process again.

The more times you go through the retrieving process, the easier it will get. You will have to run with your puppy less and less until eventually he just comes back on his own. Dropping the toy for you becomes automatic and won't take so long. The final goal is not to have the leash to help pull your puppy back and to be able to throw long distances. Remember, teaching your puppy this game is a great use of time. The dog gets lots of exercise, and it's a fun pastime for you both.

How to Make Your Puppy Stop Digging

Digging is a common behavioral problem in dogs that can be fueled by an assortment of different things. The first thing you need to know when solving this problem is that your puppy is not doing this out of spite or just to make you mad. Therefore, there should be no scolding or punishment involved, and it won't help anyway.

To solve a digging problem, the first move is to diagnose the reason. There are five common reasons:

- Your puppy has too much pent up energy
- Your puppy is bored
- Your puppy is seeking attention
- Your puppy wants comfort or shelter
- Your puppy is trying to escape

Too much energy
This is the most common cause for your puppy's digging. Sometimes people think that leaving your puppy outside gives her enough exercise, but this is not the case. If you leave your puppy unattended and full of energy in the yard, then she is bound to dig and stir up trouble. The obvious solution for this is to get your puppy more exercise. Try retrieving, walking, and swimming with your puppy. A tired puppy is a good puppy.

Bored
Another leading cause for digging puppies is boredom. When your puppy is left alone in the yard, she needs entertainment. The goal is to make her entertainment non-destructive, so she is not doing things like digging. The best way to create non-destructive entertainment is to leave out puppy toys to play with and chew on. Kong type toys that are filled with treats work particularly well for distracting a puppy for hours.

Seeking attention
As with most behavioral problems, one cause for digging is the puppy's craving for attention. If your puppy often digs when you are around, or you aren't interacting with her much, then this might be your problem. The solution to this is to be present, ignore this attention-seeking behavior, and praise her good behavior.

Seeking comfort or shelter

Another reason your puppy might dig is to protect herself from elements of nature, such as heat, cold, wind, and rain. The obvious solution for this is to either keep your puppy inside during these conditions, or to build some kind of dog house in the yard.

Escape

If the reason your puppy is digging is to escape the yard, then it should be pretty obvious to you. Just in case, though, usually the hole will be along the fence line, or under the fence. There are lots of different ways to solve this problem, but one of the most simple (and my favorite) is to puts some large rocks in the old holes before you cover them back up. This way, when your puppy digs in this spot again (and puppies often dig in the same location more than once), she will hurt her paws on the rocks and not be able to dig. After a few times, I promise your puppy will stop trying to escape.

How Dog Training Teaches Us to Communicate

Having a canine at home provides us with countless benefits for our well-being. They improve our mood. People with pets have fewer medical problems, compared to people without pets. Pets can teach kids to become more responsible. They help us reach our fitness goals and find many friends. And dogs can guard the house! These are only a few of the many benefits canines can bring us.

If your pet has some behavior issues that are bothering you, and you want to acquire all the advantages of having a pet, then it is time to tame your stubborn companion. Holistic dog training is very popular these days, since astounding results are acquired quickly. For this, research, seek out, and hire an expert trainer.

Trainers fail to achieve their goals if they are not able to communicate well with their students. Successful drills require the participation of the pet owner since the first thing that experts must gain is trust. Your dog will find it easy to trust a stranger when he sees you close to them, and you will understand your beloved pet's nature more once you've taken part in the drill. You, your pet, and your trainer must have good communication to make the process easy. Remember, your attitude has a big influence on the behavior of their pet.

Drills should be done in a place where you and your pet are comfortable. In some cases, dogs may be working on socialization, so drills are done in parks and other public places. Obedience is crucial as well. You must learn the ways of a real pack leader, so your companion will follow your commands. You must learn how to communicate, and to understand the nature of your canines fully, to initiate proper discipline. A well-behaved pet is important in a balanced society. They are meant to make our lives easier and more enjoyable, and not become a burden or a nuisance.

Dog training is critical in the puppies phase, so they will grow up to be smart and obedient companions. Building up a good foundation for them is far better than correcting behavioral problems they grew up with. Choosing a professional trainer matters a lot in the process. Good ones can change lives, and a poor trainer can make things a lot worse. Remember, anyone can advertise this service – be sure to hire from a credible company so you will have no regrets.

Know that there are reasons behind every behavioral problem, and learn to communicate with your pet to understand the underlying issue. Do not allow simple stubbornness to turn into aggression. Sometimes, successful training requires an expert. Don't hesitate to ask for help, and you will reap the benefits. Your dog will give you their unconditional love, and it is your responsibility to give back that love, and help him to reach his potential as the best pet ever.

Teach Your Dog not to Jump

Your dog uses body language and mannerisms to communicate. So when she jumps on you, she is speaking, in her way. (Likely, she's saying she's so happy to see you!) Though some people might not mind this, others realize that this behavior can be a nuisance – and even dangerous, like when she jumps on kids or guests. To eliminate this undesirable habit, you should train your dog to communicate in better ways. The following are the top strategies for putting a stop to your family dog's jumping.

Discover why dogs jump. Dog training instruction books and specialists explain that a dog jumping on someone or something is, as we have said, a way of communicating. If a dog wants to welcome someone, they jump on them to say so.

Provide the dog other ways to communicate. When you start training your dog not to jump, you will need to choose one short word, something simple which the dog will respond to, like "off" or "down." Just select one word that your dog can readily understand. Any time you give this instruction, it should be said in a firm tone, and it should not be in a high tone or too playful. Eventually, they'll associate the sound of the term and understand that they shouldn't jump.

Use body signals. Augment commands with gestures when using the "off" or "down" command. At first, without being physically punishing, you can grab his legs and pull them down to the ground. This will indicate to your puppy precisely what the down command word means, and it sends a consistent message with regards to their behavior.

Use positive encouragement. Showing your dog friendliness and affection through body gestures will show them exactly what the most appropriate communication is considered to be. Whenever they comply with the off or down command word, follow through by telling them they're right, or becoming playful in the tone of your voice. The majority of dog training guides state that this reinforces what you are expressing.

Recognize when to snarl. However, if the puppy or dog continues to disobey your "off" or "down" instruction, then try conversing using his language. Snarling and baring your teeth is a kind of communication your dog will recognize if he is doing something bad, because his mother will have done this. Whenever you do this silently, it'll tell him that you're the master, and they should obey you.

Give an explanation of the down command to your friends. A particular challenge most encounter when working with their dog is when there is a confused message in regard to the down command. Many friends or guests will allow the dog to jump on them, and are willing to have fun with the pup and may react in a playful voice. You want to make sure that everybody knows that you are training your family dog never to jump up, and additionally, advise them never to respond in a pleasant way. When your pet grows older, it may become a problem because of the dog's larger size, and the dog might jump on little children or furniture. Explain how they should react.

Solving behavioral problems with a dog is a mixture of learning the reasons they react the way they do, and interacting with them about appropriate behaviors. Using proper dog training methods can help prevent difficulties in the future. The outcome is a well-socialized dog who greets you in a civilized fashion.

How to Train Your Dog to Stay

Training your dog offers more important benefits than simply getting him or her to complete the tasks you ask. Dog training provides the opportunity to calm a hyperactive dog down, and provide more discipline in his everyday life. It also creates a bond between you, and establishes that you are the master. Proper training has far more benefits than just the actual tasks being taught.

Teaching your dog to stay is one of the first training commands you may wish to accomplish. This is a simple training method which any dog owner can teach their dog. However, do not begin the process until the dog is 8-12 months old. Young dogs are just too rambunctious for this type of training.

To begin with, find some dog treats that your dog likes and which can be stored in your pocket for easy access. One of my favorite treats for dog training are the cheese puffballs which can be purchased in any supermarket. There is no need to buy the brand name products; the inexpensive generic brands are just as well-liked by your dog as the expensive kind.

Stock your pockets with the treats, fasten a leash to your dog's collar, and head out the door into the front yard. Walk him around for a while to burn off any excess energy. Training is always easier when your dog is a bit tired. Depending on the animal, it may require a long walk before the training session even begins.

Walk the dog to the center of the yard and stop. It's best to make him sit by merely pushing his rear to the ground if he has not yet been trained to that command. If he obeys your command to sit, of course, offer him a treat right away with some rubbing. Now slacken the leash so there is no tension in it, and hold the palm of your hand in front of the dog's face and at the same time say with a firm voice, "Stay."

At that point keep holding the leash, but slowly walk backward one or two steps while extending the palm of your hand still pointing towards the dogs face. If the dog remains sitting there even for a moment, immediately return to him and praise him. Give him a treat and pet his ears. Repeat this process several times until it seems to be working well.

In the beginning, you will hold onto the leash and just back up a step or two. But as the dog progresses, you work up to the point where you will drop the leash and step back three or four paces. Gradually increase the distance and the time the dog is required to sit there before praising him. Do this for approximately 10 minutes each day for the first week. Gradually you can work up a time to 15 or 20 minutes of training each day. Also, over the coming weeks and months, you'll find you can walk farther and farther from the dog and keep him sitting there for longer periods of time. Almost all dogs are easily trainable in this fashion.

The Best Way to Keep Your Dog Healthy

When you get a dog, whether as a puppy or an adult, this animal becomes your responsibility. Most domestic dogs are unable to survive without the assistance of humans, and in addition to food and attention, your dog's health will be one of the most important aspects of dog ownership. Always remember that dogs are unable to tell you when they are feeling ill or hurt, and some breeds are so stoic (mastiff breeds especially) that they will not show that they are in trouble until they are extremely ill. It is up to the owner not only to schedule vaccinations and checkups, but also to observe their dog for any deviation from normal behavior, even if it is slight.

When you have decided upon a breed of dog, it is best to use a reputable breeder with a solid reputation. Make sure that you visit the breeder's facility and meet the puppy's parents; this will give you a good indication of the pup's future temperament. I would also recommend looking at the puppy's pedigree. Although many breeders extol the value of 'line breeding' where cousins and sometimes siblings are bred to one another repeatedly, this is still inbreeding and can cause genetic problems such as hip dysplasia, Von Willebrand disease (a form of hemophilia), Cushing's Disease, and cardiomyopathy. Make sure that the breeder's dogs are as free as possible of genetic problems, and ask to see test results.

The puppy you buy should already have been wormed and received its first vaccinations. Observe the puppies at the kennel – the one you want will be sturdy in physical appearance, and active. A hyperactive puppy will likely be a hyperactive dog, and a puppy that hides rather than coming out to meet you is also exhibiting abnormal behavior. The mental health of the puppy is every bit as important as the physical, so a pup that comes out to greet you without being frantic about it is exhibiting normal, healthy puppy behavior.

Vaccinations against common and serious canine diseases are necessary from the time a dog is a puppy. Vaccinations work by using either attenuated or dead viruses or bacteria to 'train' the immune system to fight a disease, should the dog be exposed to it. Your veterinarian will begin to vaccinate your puppy at about 6-8 weeks of age, usually beginning with a 4-way shot that will offer protection against distemper, parvo, hepatitis, and parainfluenza. If you live where leptospirosis is present, your pup will get a 5-way shot.

One of the most serious and dangerous viral diseases is rabies. This is a disease of the central nervous system which affects the brain, causing hallucinations, headache, and eventually death. It is spread by bite and can spread from dogs to humans. Rabies vaccinations will prevent the disease and are given, initially, every year, then every three years. If you are worried about the cumulative effect of rabies vaccine on your dog, it is possible to have a blood test done to make sure that your dog is still producing antibodies against the rabies virus.

Checkups for your dog are very important. A yearly (or twice yearly) checkup will not only ensure that your dog is current on all his or her vaccinations, but it will enable your vet to spot problems before they become serious. A comprehensive checkup should include complete blood work that will establish a baseline for your dog's liver and kidney functions. Should your dog become ill later, this will help your veterinarian see how much deviation has occurred.

A checkup will also allow your vet to check your dog's teeth to see if a cleaning or extractions are needed. Plaque buildup on teeth has been linked to heart and kidney disease in dogs. You can help keep the dog's teeth cleaner between checkups by either brushing them or using a damp washcloth to clean them regularly.

A healthy dog will not only be a more pleasant companion, but will also remain your companion for a longer time.

How to Introduce a New Dog into a Dog-Filled Home

The fact that you have conscientiously considered a dog's social needs does not require you to hastily introduce new dogs to the one you are currently taking care of at home. Yes, dogs need company beyond inanimate pet supplies, discounted or not; they also need the company of fellow dogs. However, the introduction has to be carefully and wisely done.

How can you carefully and wisely introduce your dog to a newcomer which you would like to add to your household? Below are among the most important pointers you could ever know about this subject.

1. **The introduction is easiest when done at puppy stage**. It's best if your dog learns to love the company of other dogs while she is still young. At this stage, everything around her seems normal, and so it won't be such an intrusion to see another puppy living with her. You only need to be fair to each puppy, especially when it comes to the

distribution of dog food, dog toys, and other things. This helps make the introductory experience very pleasant.

2. **The introduction of a new, grown dog to your currently single grown dog will be of medium difficulty.** The pride or egocentrism that has grown in the old dog will be the most challenging thing to this introduction. It should be remembered, though, that the new dog to be introduced also has this pride developed within him. It will take time for the two to accept each other's characteristics and personalities. Preparatory stages to this point would include introducing smells. You might try to spread the smell of the new dog in your home before the dog comes in. This could mean rubbing a cloth on the new dog, and then rubbing that cloth onto the sofas or the existing dog spaces.

3. **The introduction of a new dog to a family of well-acquainted home dogs might be the most challenging**. This is particularly true for the reasons stated in the previous case, and also because of the close ties already formed among the old dogs. There will have to be social acceptance, or there can be a division that forms among your older pets. This case will take much patience, and thus the introduction has to be made more gradually. One effective technique is to occasionally walk the old dogs, and have some other companion lead the new one, this to be done in a public place, such as the park. If they can make friends outside the house, it will become easier for the old dogs to welcome the new friend as a housemate.

Your Dog's Biggest Problem, and How to Solve It

There is no magic solution, but you can change your dog's annoying behavior. It doesn't help you much now to tell you that the best way to deal with bad behavior in your dog is to prevent it in the first place. People spend time researching and buying a car and then maintaining it. They will spend hours planning a vacation. They send their kids to school for more than 180 days a year for no less than 12 years. But when it comes to their dog, they think it all should just work out somehow.

Dogs need to be properly trained in the first place, and then most of the problems we encounter will not even happen. But it might be even more important to train the owner! How many dog owners have never even read a book or watched a video on how to relate to their pet? I know you don't want to hear this, but most problem behavior with your pet is your fault, not your dog's. Like Cesar Millan, the "Dog Whisperer" and TV personality, likes to say, he trains people and he rehabilitates dogs.

In many cases the biggest problem with your dog is that you have let him be in charge. He thinks he is running things, or he is anxious because you are clearly not in charge. It's often not that your dog wants to be the leader, it's just that someone has to be, and he's pretty sure it's not you right now.

You can love your dog and still be the boss. Dogs, like children, need to have a leader. They don't want to be in charge. They want someone to show them the boundaries and direct them. They want to have rules and structure. In the wild, dogs have a pack leader who provides for them, protects them, and sets rules and boundaries. In your world, that pack leader needs to be you. But if you don't do it, your dog probably will.

Yes, your dog does need affection, but that is not his greatest need. You want to just love him and comfort him and snuggle with him. However, in doing only that, you are causing him more harm than good. Discipline and exercise must come above affection. Then the affection has much greater meaning.

The other thing most dogs are lacking that contributes to their unwanted behavior is exercise. The typical household pet gets little to none of this each day. Just letting your dog out into the backyard for a few minutes doesn't count. When he's been cooped up all day alone, he needs a long walk – or better still – a run. A lot of behavior problems would simply vanish if the pet had adequate exercise. He is then better prepared to follow your leadership.

The point is, if we do our part, that goes a long way towards solving our pet's behavior problems. It doesn't do any good at this point to beat ourselves up because we could have avoided the misbehavior in the first place. Our dog has developed some habits that need to be changed. But even if the dog's problematic behavior is dealt with and corrected, unless we make changes in the way we relate to him, it will probably not solve the problem permanently.

Here are some tips on how to establish yourself as the boss, as the pack leader.

1. Work on developing a "positive-assertive" attitude. It never helps to yell at your dog. Being upset only bothers you, and does little to correct your dog's behavior.

Watch and control how you react toward your pet. He will sense your inner attitude. You need to determine and believe that you are in charge, and not him. Then be positive, concentrating on what you want instead of what you don't want.

2. Do not overreact. Monitor your behavior and think before you respond. Just as with children, usually your first reaction to a bad situation is the wrong one. So stop and think before you act.

3. Do not comfort your dog or offer him affection at the wrong times. When he is acting out of fear or anxiety he doesn't need comforting, he needs a positive-assertive leader. Save the affection and "mothering" for when his behavior is what you desire, not when he is misbehaving. What you reward will be repeated.

4. When you feed your dog, make him get permission before he eats. Don't allow him to rush you and grab the food. Make him sit and stay while you prepare and deliver the food. Make him wait a minute or two, just to prove who's in charge. Then tell him "okay," and he can eat.

5. When you open the door, do not allow him to run out. Make him sit and wait until you tell him he may go out. Again, prove who's boss and release him when you are ready, not when he is impatient. It won't hurt to make him wait until he settles down some.

6. Go first. If you are going outside with your dog, you always go out the door first, or in the door first. Who goes first: the pack leader or the followers?

7. Be consistent. Teach your dog basic commands, enforce them, and require that your entire family be consistent with his training and behavior. If each family member does something different with the dog, he only becomes confused and anxious. Dog training must be a family lifestyle.

So if there's a problem with the dog, then first, we need to look at ourselves and how we react and relate to her. Then we will be ready to deal with the bad habits and go to the next step in a wonderful and rewarding relationship with our best friend.

~

In summary, dogs tend to be fun-loving, lovable, and make very good companions. When properly trained, they are good pets for almost any person. When you keep in mind the advice from this book, your dog will soon be properly trained and an adorable companion for you.

Photography Credits

Also by Lou Jefferson

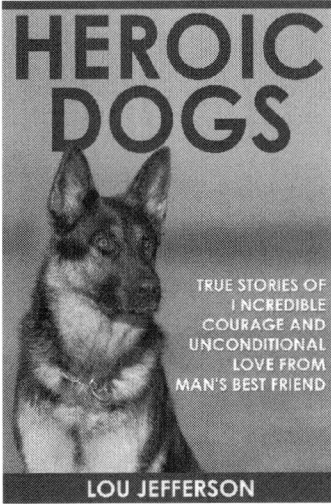

HEROIC DOGS
TRUE STORIES OF INCREDIBLE COURAGE AND UNCONDITIONAL LOVE FROM MAN'S BEST FRIEND
LOU JEFFERSON

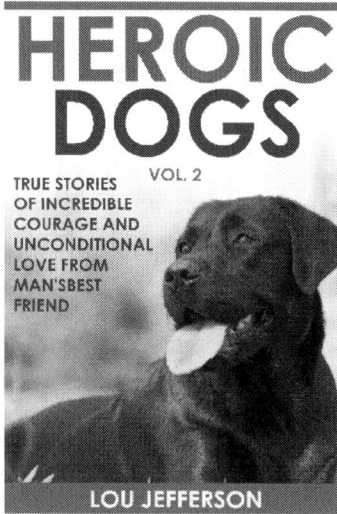

HEROIC DOGS VOL. 2
TRUE STORIES OF INCREDIBLE COURAGE AND UNCONDITIONAL LOVE FROM MAN'S BEST FRIEND
LOU JEFFERSON

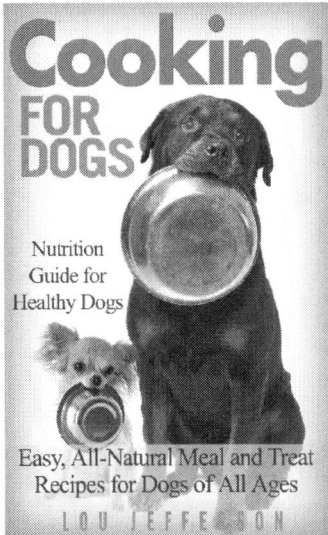

Cooking FOR DOGS
Nutrition Guide for Healthy Dogs
Easy, All-Natural Meal and Treat Recipes for Dogs of All Ages
LOU JEFFERSON

Printed in Great Britain
by Amazon